GREEN IGUANAS

by Imogen Kingsley

AMICUS | AMICUS INK

Amicus High Interest and Amicus Ink are published by Amicus
P.O. Box 1329, Mankato, MN 56002
www.amicuspublishing.us

Library of Congress Cataloging-in-Publication Data
Names: Kingsley, Imogen, author.
Title: Green iguanas / by Imogen Kingsley.
Description: Mankato, Minnesota : Amicus/Amicus Ink, [2019] | Series:
   Lizards in the wild | Audience: K to Grade 3. | Includes index.
Identifiers: LCCN 2018004176 (print) | LCCN 2018006678 (ebook) | ISBN
   9781681515960 (pdf) | ISBN 9781681515588 (library binding) | ISBN
   9781681523965 (paperback)
Subjects: LCSH: Green iguana--Juvenile literature.
Classification: LCC QL666.L25 (ebook) | LCC QL666.L25 K56 2019 (print) |
   DDC 597.95/42--dc23
LC record available at https://lccn.loc.gov/2018004176

Photo Credits: Shutterstock/y blue-sea.cz, cover, tratong, 2, 22, Colin D.
Young, 6, Renat Murtaev, 10, Kuznetsov Alexey, 13, Angel Dibilio, 14;
Alamy/Rob Crandall, 5, Arto Hakola, 17, Alejandro Díaz Díez, 21; iStock/
passion4nature, 9; Getty/Danita Delimont, 18

Editor: Mary Ellen Klukow
Designer: Peggie Carley
Photo Researcher: Holly Young

Printed in China

HC 10 9 8 7 6 5 4 3 2 1
PB 10 9 8 7 6 5 4 3 2 1

TABLE OF CONTENTS

A BIG LIZARD

The green iguana is big! It
can be over 6 feet (1.8 m)
long. It is the biggest lizard
in the United States. It eats
leaves. It eats flowers.

WHERE THEY LIVE

Green iguanas live in Mexico and Florida. They also live in Central and South America. They live in **rainforest** trees. They like to be by water.

Check This Out
An iguana spends almost all its time in trees.

A GOOD SWIMMER

An iguana climbs down from its tree. It runs to the water. It moves its body side to side. It is a good swimmer!

Check This Out
A green iguana can stay underwater for 30 minutes.

NOT JUST GREEN

Many green iguanas are green.

They come in other colors, too.

Some are orange, blue, or pink.

Like all reptiles, they have **scales**.

A LONG TAIL

An iguana has a long tail. Its tail is half the length of its body. It can use it like a whip against attackers. If its tail breaks off during an attack, it can grow a new one.

SPINES AND CLAWS

A green iguana has long claws.
They dig. They grip. It has spines
down its back. If it is being hunted,
it will put up its spines. Then it
looks big and scary.

THE MALE

A male bobs his head up and down. He looks up and shows his **dewlap**. This extra flap of skin hangs from his neck. What is he doing? He is looking for a female.

DIGGING
A NEST

A female likes the way he looks.
They **mate**. Soon she digs a
nest. Her back legs push rocks
away. Her front claws dig. She
goes into the **burrow**.

YOUNG IGUANAS

The female lays many eggs. Then she leaves. In three months, the eggs hatch. The **hatchlings** poke out. They are ready to explore.

Check This Out
A female lays 10 to 76 eggs at a time!

A LOOK AT A GREEN IGUANA

spines

tail

dewlap

claws

WORDS TO KNOW

burrow An underground home or nest.

dewlap A flap of skin under a lizard's neck.

hatchling A young lizard.

mate When a male and female come together to make babies.

rainforest A tropical forest with tall trees that gets a lot of rain.

scales Hard, thin plates that cover a reptile's skin.

LEARN MORE

Books

Black, Vanessa. *Green Iguanas*. Minneapolis: Bullfrog Books, 2017.

Bodden, Valerie. *Iguanas*. Mankato, Minn.: Creative Education, 2017.

Duhaime, Darla. *Iguanas*. Vero Beach, Flor.: Rourke, 2017.

Websites

Active Wild: Facts About Iguanas
https://www.activewild.com/facts-about-iguanas/

DK Find Out!: Lizards
https://www.dkfindout.com/us/animals-and-nature/reptiles/lizards/

San Diego Zoo: Lizards
http://animals.sandiegozoo.org/animals/lizard

INDEX